Year of the Dog

Selected as one of the country's Next Generation poets, shortlisted for the 2004 Sunday Times Young Writer of the Year and named by the *TLS* as one of the best young writers in the country, Tobias Hill is one of the leading British writers of his generation. His award-winning collections of poetry are *Midnight in the City of Clocks*, *Zoo* and *Nocturne in Chrome & Sunset Yellow*, all available from Salt. His fiction has been published to acclaim in many countries. A.S. Byatt has observed that "There is no other voice today quite like this."

Also by Tobias Hill

Year of the Dog

TOBIAS HILL

CAMBRIDGE

PUBLISHED BY SALT PUBLISHING
PO Box 937, Great Wilbraham, Cambridge CB21 5JX United Kingdom

© Tobias Hill, 1995, 2007

The right of Tobias Hill to be identified as the
author of this work has been asserted by him in accordance
with Section 77 of the Copyright, Designs and Patents Act 1988.

First published by National Poetry Foundation 1995
This edition Salt Publishing 2007

Printed and bound in the United Kingdom by Biddles Ltd, King's Lynn, Norfolk

Typeset in Swift 9.5 / 13

ISBN 978 1 84771 415 5 hardback

Salt Publishing Ltd gratefully acknowledges
the financial assistance of Arts Council England

1 3 5 7 9 8 6 4 2

For Xandra

Contents

Acknowlededgments

Acknowledgements are due to the editors of the following publications in which some of the poems in this collection first appeared: *Apostrophe, Bare Bones, Connections, Dial 174, Envoi, The Independent, London Magazine, Northwords, The Observer, Odyssey, Outposts, Pause, Printed Matter, Sepia, Smiths Knoll, Stand, Staple, Supperreal, Symphony, Tabla, Understanding.*

Poems from this collection have been anthologised by Beehive, BMI, Bridport Press publications and Staple First editions, and have appeared in poster form from the BMI and the Kitley Trust.

London Pastoral

There's something I've wanted to show you. Here—
between derelicts:
a bomb-chink of brake-lights.

Ice? More? Just say when.
Open the corrugated paper
of these lung-machine blinds;
sun slides across the floor,
contained as yolk-skin.

Unlock the mortice-lock and pause and swing open
wide windows. Seagulls on the curry-house
scream of distance with the coices
of illegal aliens. Hold onto your fluted glass.

I want to tell you something:
for three nights now a bird has sung
in the road trees. A water song.
The neighbours are complaining; no one
knows what species the bird is. No one
even sees it. Pools coupons
titter against chain-links. Chip cartons
scuttle past time-delayed,
time-locked shopfronts. Then the bird
starts to sing.

You'll hear it with the window open,
even when the first rain gathers
to a downpour, hallways sweet
with the residue of road-tar.
Then you can grin, or watch me grin
at woodpigeons in wet weather
sat in the road trees, suffering
damp white collars. Like divorcees,
not looking at one another.

Close

The cockroaches are rain-skittish.
They ruin like condensations
from foundation-cracks, stumble and flex
their wings. One flies like a stone.
Grandmother Kamate, pickling white radishes,
claps the beetle to her breast
when it falls there. She mutters, tuts
at the sky. Wipes her loose skin
with a Kleenex, shooes her grandchildren
outside. Tightens her house-kimono, then
open her *Lucky Strikes* and smokes.

Outside, I sit uncomfortably
by Mr Kim's Nissan, watching
the granchildren wrestle and sing.
Aeroplanes are disguised as thunder,
thunder as the slop and buckle
of rain in bucckets of clouds
waiting for a door to open.
Dogs yip, echo
like dophin song. Cicadas
rant small raindancs. The smell
of pennies and oysters,

electric. Rain; always gives me
that howling feeling. Times to check
my watch, bus timestables, or
wire Mr Kim;s car and drive,

air so close to tender skin
it comes alive, and just behind,
rain creeping like an edge of char
across pages of maps and horizons.

The Mosquito's Opposite

Such a brilliant weapon
spawned from the dull clay-cool of a water jar
or from an oil-lacquered puddle.

Improved to its place like a stone
in a sea. In a ring, faceted. A brilliant thing.

Its blueprint, scribbled in amber,
is unaltered. The conceived form
near-perfect, never improved upon. The line
surer than Picasso's circle, fine
as a shark's teeth, a flatworm's gut,
the unbreakable fractal of a fern.

The vibration of its wings
figures in dreams as the whine
of a dentists's drill, the songs of glass
and the air-raid siren, or
a small child weeping. Alone
and the walls listening.

There's almost nothing to it. Blood,
no heart. The broken drift of legs
under the rubber stomach, where
the forms of life less familiar
latch and grow towards release.

Permanence and its opposite:
the host, the virus antigen

shifting from face to grotesque face
down in the heartbeat of the blood.

Waiting

Before morning I'm aiting here,
drinking green tea by the red door.
In my pocket there are keys,
two pens, one emptied. One of the keys
opens a box in England. In the box
is my grandfather's microscope,

with iris-valves that wink and dilate
like snake-eyes, and chipped glass sides
of a sexless baby's head
small as my watch-face; a foetus —

this is irrelevant. This is
relevant. the nigth sky

goes down behind Wu's Viking Grill
And Beer Hall. Clouds move
like mountains. I wait.
Across Seven Stone Children Street
the fishmonger's son carries tuna
by the cheeks, hoooks up cabs.
He looks them over with the care
of a potter. Sour ash

lifts from the icing factory.
I scribble margin-notes. a bloody rash
of water spreads from the butcher's door.
The match-scratch of the first cicada
ignites the sun. By twelve o'clock

it's a cymbal-crash
in the high branches. My knuckles crack, hands
on the page, waiting to cut
the ventricles and heat of noon
with the tremor of a pen.

[4]

In the Rooms of the Plague House

When summer comes, no-one is left
to halt the termites' veiny roads
before the bridge the villa doors
ans populate the shanty-towns. Nothing is felt
when ribbed dogs fight
for bones under the collonades
and on-one hears the bell-beetles
stringing the dusk with telephones.

The inmates of the fine white house
are gone. Theer is a rusty smear
of bloodthe doctors would not touch
where the last carrier was shot.
The daughter, whose honey-black hair
was striped s the hips of a bee,
moves like fish-skin in hte harbour.
Phosphorescence haloes her.

Some of them diied in secret,
most were killed. Virus excites virus.
Arrangements of flowers and salt
were left inside the airless rooms.
They hide the emergence of rot.
The windows crossed and nailed shut.

entropy gains momentum. Blood
is split into constituents,
protein, iron, and sold off
to white ants and Red Admirals.
The stink of ozone in the street
is overcome by the cesspit gas.
The petrol-station creaks under
the whisky-gold dynamit sun,

explodes. The white house is charred black.
The rain steams and polishes it
smooth as a cenotaph's granite.

Inside the multiscreen, left on,
has fused the complicated script
of circuitry behind the walls.
A lithium-cell radio
reports the plague's progress North-East,
the virus already global,
a myth. Discussed but never thought.

the flower ases in the hall
are Edo period and Lalique,
nthing stolen. Nothing touched.
In the infant and child ward,
by trestles, convolvulus
contract,

lungs fighting for breath,
dustless as skin.

In the plague house
the children wait for vaccination,
sitting still, knuckles white.

The Secret of Burning Diamonds

Bought from the marts of Amsterdam
the city built on herring-bones,
where emeralds dug in Ceylon
glitered and still smelt of oysters—

this one was the first to burn,
a diamond ugly and flat—
lustred as a cod's eye. the size
of a black-olive stone, or so,
smelling of mine-mud. flawed at heart,
the Jews of Rialto gauged it
(their wives and daughters topaz-eyed),
and wouldn't pawn it for as shirt.

not for the rose-cut, that one, tough
stubborn-ugly. Its chandelier
hatchmarked withi cracks and despite that
the strongest substance in the world:
diamond. A lock for alchemists
to break. A Bluebeard's Door, a fear.

A courtyard in Florence. Lenses
and barrels make a microscope
bigger than siege-cannons. The jewel
under the glass, set in steel.

On the clothes of the audience,
a whiff of morning markets, sweat
and pomanders. Cedar, olives,
with branches like green bronze. the sun
rising. Noteworthy men, thinkers,
waiting to vivisect their God
under the momentum of light.

Apex. Strengthening in the lens,
a rift of noon. The diamond
smokes—

wonder! The prince or the Dauphin
whispers profanities. Hisses
of proofs and miracles
and the crack of an atom,
the dam-burst of flame—

a miracle. The purest jewel
reduced to dust.

A Year in Japan

The newsapers, chained to the rack,
could be today's or yeterday's;
I cannot read what day it is.
I sit beside the hotel clock
and watch the certainty of time.

The hotel ashtray-cleaner
brings me green rice-cakes
wrapped in veined leaves.
They smell of fish and nicotine.
Tokyo fills the window's frame.

The towers and the groundscrapers
excrete vapour and in the rain
a rush-hour of bicycles
threads the stop-lights. The sky is grey,
blank. A dead computer-screen.
the horizon is fused with smog.

A Chinese girl with orange hair
sits crosslegged by the TV.
She channel-surfs. Monsters, baseball,
game shows and samurai blend
into montage, are suddenly lost
in a tide-hiss of static snow.

I wake. Night. A chameleon worm
of subway train turns gold and green
between two love-hotels, burrows
under a Coca-Cola sign.
the traffic's spine of tail-lights
slows by the pinball palaces
where neon dragons leap and dive.

The girl with orange hair is gone.
The computer has come alive.

FEBRUARY

At six my rooms shake when the train
rocks by. Its cables flash and sway
before it comes after it's gone.
Doors swing. the kitchen clock falls like a bomb.

I go looking for coffee,
needing it, and not really knowing
if there is coffee in Japan.
Along the streets, shops are shut up
behind locked grills till ten o'clock.

Only the all-night store's awake,
spilling white neon on the lot
where old men in white pantaloons
sit and chat like radios
in the half-dark, not listening.

Monologues on their past loves.
The fishmonger opens for business.
Lifts the skin off the back of a salmon
with the skill of a killer reomving his gloves.

I sit alone in the public garden
drinking coffee from a can,
enjoy its bitterness alone,

listening to the crickets' scratch
like telephones in empty rooms.

MARCH

For my birthday, roast sparrow
and saké from a blue bottle.

Under the concrete viaduct
the white dog of the carpenter
barks into its own echo.

It's market day outside the shrine.
Bruised arcs of prawns and ruddy knots
of octopus. A steel plate
of mullet heads. A wooden tub
of elvers, flexing
and reflexing.

Between the factories and maize
the flowers of the plum ripen
from sapling green to barest hint
of blood. The hunchbacked women work
among te figs, their hammer-blows
a skip before the hammer-beats.

By city hall, salarymen
throw rice at the tail-thrust
and ripple of black carp
in the frozen pool,
echoes in a mirror.

APRIL

Noon. In its sleep theh earth turns over
with the ease of eels in a bucket;
oily, muscular. Schoolchildren

brake their bikes. Beside the road a cockerel
cocks his rusted plumes,
goes on digging with his spurs
into garbage. A farmworker
leans on her adze, watches him,
her cheek cuddling chewing-gum.
grinning. Clothes lacquered smooth with dirt.

My rooms shudder again, when
the couple in the flat upstairs
make love. Once in a month, almost
without a sound. face to the wall.
He's unemployed. before lunchtime
he wakes. Lights up. Turns on the news.

A night, lamplit zeppelins
roll overhead like harvest moons,
advertising abalone
and rice. I walk with eyes to the ground,
avoiding cracks. Testing the stone.

MAY

Spring in the rush-hour train:
the ticket-man, sumo-fat
and hurrying. The frills of his uniform
confettied with blossom.
Cherry in the hat-band, plum dark
in the splendid epaulettes.

Sunlight blinks between the hulks
of love-hotels. A pyramid, a Palace
of Versailles. Balconies
on the Garden Babylon
backlit, ivy polythene green.

The businessman in the next seat
reads graphic erotica. Holds the book
in both hands. In each strip
vamps and rapes, demons. Thick
as a Shakespeare. He doesn't look
at the girl in the seat opposite,

though I watch her, safely sleeping.
Head back, and the sun filming
her face. How the eyebrows are raised
when she dreams. And beyond her, small
in a landscape of water,

the flash of a kingfisher
taking a clean kill
like a lit crack in carnival glass.

JUNE

After eight days the fall eases.
Roof-tiles shine, blue as a bruise.
The white noise of rain season
stops. Rooks cough in the hush.

The crops are plastered to the mud
like sodden hair against a forehead.
The hammered clods
glazed with white clouds.

Smog begins to gather round
the neon of the gambling halls
and the arclights of factories. It tastes of iron,
garlic, burnt, its compound changing on the tongue.

Evening. In the sun's first long gleam
the sky's measure is taken in
by the reach of the rainbow. Schoolboys ride home
against the rising wind, taking their time.
Their girls lean into them, sidesaddle.
Wide skirts and black hair
flying. The air glitters with dragonflies.

Hidden by bar-room gloom
I envy them the moment,
jealous of their discoveries.

JULY

Sweat cools to a sheen
on skin and asphalt.
Gravel as warm as teeth in a mouth.

It stays that way, when the red earth
and troutskin sky register only
as terms of grey. Noon's aftershock.
Streetlights wink on, paid out straight
into the street's vanishing-point.

In the calligrapher's backyard,
by yesterday's picked herring-bones,
boulders erode. Their seams of quartz
the white tusks of a mastodon.

Sweat cools. Under my palm
the page spread, and the writing-brush
a teardrop of black ink. I write
the characters for poem, sun.
Foreign and incompetent. Again.
Dip the brush. Rest it light.

Outside, the children play, pollen
from sunflowers and white moth-wings
dulling the darker stains of ink.

Two languages. Characters in
the flue of water and the flow
of limbs. Their language, a their feet.
Words in the script of rooftops, roots,
letters shaped to the fold of a bough.
In dust and the wide eye of the mind,

Pages gathered to the path of the wind.

AUGUST

Between the rag-slap of docks
and the winch-creak of abbatoirs,
she stops talking. In pairs,
alone, the warehouse men
go home. Quiet, faces down.

Later, the saké warm as milk,
she finds the word for them. "Untouchable."
"How could you tell?" She rubs her hands,
washing, "Their bones. Eyes. Differences."
Their name means *Waste People*. They work
with blood, the filth of animals.

Summer: season of poisonings.
In the space of hours, kept meat
colours, rainbows on asphalt tar.
Eggs are sucked light with hidden rot.
Crack open to a curd of gold.
The fishmonger drinks turtles' blood,
it washes the heart clean and strong;
he recommends it, as he guts.

Evening. Next door a snakeskin hangs
nailed over the windowframe, drifts
in the wind. Poison for ghosts
and sickness. The mosquitoes whine.
Quiet, when it comes, is
only the presence of intent.

Down by the docks and abbatoirs
the workers sit by the sea-shrine,
dreaming of summer in Japan.
Sweating with slight fever, heads bent,
waiting for the night-shift siren.

SEPTEMBER

Their bodies red as fishing-floats,
dragonflies bask by the outposts
of a U.S. Army base, bunting
strung along perimeters.
In typhoon season the razor-wire,
suspended tight as lute-stings,
shrieks like an accident,
fills the air with its wings.

On Sunday, the fishmonger's window
has been jewelled overnight
with frogs. Duck-neck green, bellied with gold.
They are the last to go, dug back
into thick cauls of paddy-mud.
I wake from dreams of deafness
to the loss of frog-song.

Night has become a quiet time,
the earth a motor cooling, cold.
Bats navigating
on the far edge of sound.

OCTOBER

She meets the train
at Burning Stone station,
red leaves in her pocket
and the river from the mountain
green as an eye.

The sun keeps rhythm
through the pines. The train beats time. She tells me that
her names translate as Three Eight Sweet One,
Sickle-Hand, and that her town
is famous for carrots, and that

the moon has no face in Japan,
but the shadow of a hare, leapt
from the arms of a god.

Later, under the sod-black trees
she hides her face against the wind
and asks me to teach her to kiss.

NOVEMBER

By the subway exit
the tramp with watchmaker's hands
has gone on his rounds, leaving
three magazines, five blankets, folded small
under the granite statue
of Persephone in Hell.

He's from Beijing. Sometimes he writes
Chinese characters on her breasts.
At eight-fifteen, the rush-hour
bottlenecks, to read the words.

He cleans her skin
himself, rubbing mica flecks
with back-pages of newspaper.
Reads them and then sogs them
in the computerised fountain.
He stands by its corkscrewed chrome,
waiting for water to come
and the snowflakes fat as cornflakes.

I watch him form the park's interior,
behind the temple. No noise
but the slew of a car, the snow's clomp
falling from trees
and from the kindergarten

the sound of mass hysteria.

December

The tranquillity—
no cars. Green soaks
into ice on the traffic-lights,
slithers to red. New Year's Eve,
full of the sound of temple bells.

I cool. She comes late with presents.
Black eyelashes, white snow. Ice-cream.
A wrist-watch that glows in the dark
like a moon paralyzed in fullness.

My flight is booked. Tokyo, London.
We eat. We try, now, not to ask
too many questions. At night
she takes my hand in hers and pulls
the quilt over her head, to see.
The time between us, when we kiss.

There are few endings. Death, the twist.
happiness, sadness, Modernist. There are
so few good endings. Now,
snow thaws to rain and falls. The year
ends as the second-hand steps past
in its luminous dark, black
as a wasp's foot. I brew
green tea, drink it and sleep restless,
dreaming of failures, laughter
Carnival. The Underground.

Four. The dead hour. From the hulk
of Morinaga's Factory
the smell of cooking caramel, its warmth
soft in the cold air and the earth
frozen to asphalt. I walk.
The trees hare, their grasping hands
full of moon's milk.

Snake Oil

Always three steps ahead
of fashion, she wears
reflective contact lenses.
Standing in the mirror's vault
she stares into infinity.
She takes them out only
to screw, but wears them
when she sleeps and dreams.

Along the tendons of her heels
rose tattoos in UV ink.
Later, she'll be dancing barefoot,
the petals lit under strobelights.
She paints her nails, pouts
snake oil. Plays for another drink.

In the grey trudge of dawn
she slips between the first cars,
teeth on edge with speed, vitamin K,
lock-jawed. She sleeps to ease the hit,
with the white noise of the TV left on.
Sometimes, though her eyes are barred
with mirrors, there will be a word,

a sentence-fragment from the lives
of a watchful family. The slender knives
of silences. Expectations, the lurch
of shame. The hide
and seek. The butterflies
trapped without ever knowing
in the summer-house's oven.

She takes their glassy wings,
rouges her cheeks with dead pollen.

A mother's voice calling to church
and the breath of the girl. Running, running.

Night-Ride, Japan

Late-shift done and only the bike
for company. Grease cold, the chain
clanks like a gun factory
and the tundra of rice-fields
page-blank, the snow hardening

to a script of ice. Just here, last night,
the back brake snapped. Popped like a tendon, when
I slewed to watch a star's track, wept
from the blind face of Orion.

Like a firework, but sleet-thin
with distance. At the edge of air.
I tried to wish before it flamed
down to a pebble, out of sight. Rare dust.
Now the dynamo grinds its teeth
and gutters light.

I stop and wait, head back, to catch
snow on the tongue. Its purity
reeks of pollutions. Cold oil, essence
of memory. The smell of a tyre-swing
over a river,

a car-crash in Columbia. Cyanide-stench
of gas,. Burnt rubber. Fish and chips
in a London gutter. Cod-skin,
headline ink and vinegar

The sky clears
suddenly. Lights wink
up on the radar towers
and the car factories. With one eye
crescent and mad,
Orion stares.

On the Island of Pearls

(In memory of Kokichi Mikimoto, inventor of the cultured pearl)

Along the jetty, sparrows nag
at the green shells of plum blossom
still clenched, and the sea-sky
luminous as the nape of an abalone.

Something was invented here.
We tour boutiques and show-rooms, where
days are measured out in strands,
their length, lustre. Weeks in the sphere
of one perfect pearl. An organic jewel
that comes in all the colours of the skin.

Something was invented. So many kinds
of failure: the Odd, the Butterfly, the Twin,
which grows into an hourglass.
The Lobe and Tongue, grotesqueries,
worthless. Pain embalming itself like wax
dropped down the candle's shank.
The pearl is a function of pain.

In the next room, a young woman
sits between baroque sculptures;
an ocean shrine, a sea-god's crown
nacred. She bows and demonstrates
the method of insertions,
the oyster's poached skin
slit like the white of an egg. Somewhere
outer doors open, her words
drowned in the sea's yawn and boom.

The jetty smells of white salt, sunshine, plum.
We rest under massive bronze
of the Pearl King. He stands like one, eyes
setting his lands in order
through cataracts of verdigris.
Still looking for the hears, to find
always inside the immaculate pearl

dirt. The lustre of mud.
We buy rice-cakes, walk among
the blossom trees to the arcades,
hoardings on old nails screeching
in the load of the wind. The sound
sweet as bird-song.

Today the House is Full of Dishcloths

Today the house is full of dishcloths
they pad staircases and loom blue
across back doors, hung out to dry.
The yard cats have got hold of one.
They worry it and leave it scrawled
on the steps like a half-dead bird.

someone's crying in the hall,
coal-sack eyes pressed against
dishcloths. The kitchn drawers ar epacked
with four tin-openers and dishcloths
scorch-marked, soft, screen-printed
with Rutland hedgerow birds no-one
has ever heard. 'Old Father Thames Hotels'
where none of us have stayed.

At TV dinner time, no-one
asks for a serviette. We eat
tin-tray foods, emptying out
the new old freezer in the hall,
with ample dishcloths on our knees.
the house smells of asparagus
and there are smart disturbances:

Bookshelves cluttered with crocus-bulbs,
allotment onions, 'Pearl' light bulbs,
a glass car ornament, Lalique,
'Swallow drinking', fly-screwed
to a lathed length of boxwood.

Wooden coat-hangers are clumped
on door-knobs. hung from one, there is
a black waistcoat we all try on,
but which will fit no-one. the stairs
are cramped with saucer-tins of film

that tick and burn, unwinding
in a dark room, blazing light.
Catalogued in tight script,
a doctor's time-of-death handwriting—

'*Textures*'. Tor-grass, mud-ruts, mined
earth. '*Boating*'. the sun's hull, sepia
tideswells. Snapshots of family,
but always framed from distances.

It's hard to recognise faces.
Harder to search it all and find
this one fine human frailty. Here:
blurred by proximity.

My grandfather's finger
exposed in the foreground.

Rio in Carnival

The earth is hot,
the smell of blacktop
steaming in the rain is sweet
as meat and red lipstick. Coffee
and guarana churn up the guts
into an empty wakefulness.
Roosting in the breadfruit trees
the vultures scent adrenaline,
stretch the blackout of their wings.

Down by Ipanema, the beach
printed with light, curved as a thigh,
Will dances with a transvestite
from Argentina. She sings
Piaf, Marlene and the Stones,
eyes enamelled chrome-blue, too full
of keeping up appearances.

Rain for three days and without sleep,
we drink sugar-cane alcohol
with Mike from Bradford and his girl.
She plays cat's-cradle on his knees, her smile
fixed as the Queen's on watered paper.
"Look at her, see those paps,
young man. Fit as a butcher's dog. Ha!"
Through NHS black spectacles
he winks. Behind his back, the ocean
glitters, thin as caviar.

Women or men? Body-paint runs
blue vines over naked skin.
At the Grand Ball, the beautiful
arrive with godmothers, who watch
not for watchers, the poor voyeurs,
but for the nod, the finger's snap,
the crack of Washington's head on a bill.
In the wings they fix
the price of nights on calculators.

From the upper balconies,
the tourist guides and foreigners
applaud the lambada dancers,
and young bloods bow to the boxes
where old families and new men
observe from the leathered dark.
The band plays music without scores

in the pits, and the view from the gods
inked with the sepia of cigars.

Outside, we find a telephone,
call England. Happy something,
someone. Then wine from the Amazon
in rooms with golden wallpaper.
The liquor cures cancer, and burns—

Drums along Copacabana,
dealers and whores working the shades.
Where the sea ends, city begins—

Rio. The mango-man skins fruit
with a machete. Tells us God
took five days to finish this place,
one for the rest. Oil wells up from the soft flesh

and where the shanty-towns have slipped
from the hills in the slough of rain
a body in a ditch of trash
is not a tragedy for most:
death has no more drama
than poverty. Nothing worth waiting for.

Next morning we write postcards home
from the Sugar Loaf mountain
where hummingbirds turn the sun green.

Dreaming of Home

Beyond the rocks of Ephesus
the goatherd led us to a rise
of land over the distant sea;

there were a pair of tesserae,
one gold, one of a fine-grained blue,
disoreded in the wind and dust.

there was no crisis there,
there was no heart. The eye seaerched
for patterns and found only

a lame goat, sheltering
under the steep branches
of the eucalyptus,

a heelbone of the past.

Blood-red seaweeds drip
along that coast—

Not mine. Who wrote this line?
Ths isn't mine to write—

here. I am here. I am.
The moon is shining
and the frogs are singing.

Prelude
(Written in Brazil, 1989)

And as the years passed
the first fish,
flashing silver in the bright salt sun
became the fearful glitter of coin
and of the bitter wheeling seagull's eye.
Hunger and pain
and greed.

And as the short years passed
the savegery of the sea,
the rolling of the deep sea,
no longer struck fast fire
from his eyes,
or burnt thick, boiling within his sinewed veins,
but in his ears became
the howling of the thin-ribbed wolf
between cold pines.

And then
the years had passed.
Had ebbed away to the slate sea grey
within his fine blown hair.
The first fish and last
flashed like his sunbright youth
too soon lost and past.

The long years and short,
the green shallows and black deeps
washed away the flame and fire
the fierce desire which burnt but
could not last.

He was left is gaze,
fast across the dawn grey waves
the seagull's scream,
the shipmens' graves.
He was left alone
with the sea.

From the Bullet Train

At the far edge
of the arclit terminus
an old man sits in the sunlight
between his backdoor and hte tracks,
scooping white pupkin seeds
from their yellow hollow
with a black lacquer bowl.

Beside me, the businessman's wife
sleeps with her face averted
from her husband or lover,
not quite smiling. Silence
and slow motion. Her eyes open.
The pupils are
pinpoints of thought.

the carriage leans
into the curve of the track,
picking up speed. Zinc roofs
below the viaduct and blue smoke
from the piano factory—
passed in a moment. The sea
levels the horizon.

"Sashimi. Coffee or tea."
The businessman eats raw eels
from a polystyrene dish
patterned with copper clouds.
I turn. Outside

a swamp town. Sluggish flats
of rice and buckwheat.
A horse and cart.
By its mother's side the colt
running on graceless legs,
learning movement
to the sound of the wheel—

Gone. I sleep and wake only
when the businessman's wife
touches my arm. She points;
bamboo blossom, that flowers
once in every hundred years.

Sallow flowers hung
from a sheaf of spears.

On the Slow Mountain Train

Between the leather seats
the white goat bleats
at the sack that drips
salt water, clicking
with the claws and eyes
of blue crayfish –

"No more room. All clear."
With mangoes in their teeth,
the children climb the carriages
to ride bareback
across the mountain plain –

"No room!"
Links lock.
Twin tracks.
Mud ruts.
Sunlight.
Women chanting
"Peach, plantain,
plantain, mutton!"
The wheels turn
into themselves.

Ruts of sunlight travelling,
travelling ruts of sunlight

dust. On the old man's lap
a white goose, motionless
under blue hands
that stroke, caress.
Swaying with the carriages.
Stench of alpaca and sweat.

We drink sugar-cane alcohol
that dries the air
until no air is left. He grimaces.
"This is the Devil's Railway."
The goat-woman, head back, drinking.

"Because it falls from heaven?"
Laughter. He grins
with rusting teeth,
rocking, rocking.

"Because the Devil rides this train."

Outside, the sky dulls
black smoke
a mane of soot

valiant dust. The crayfish hiss
with pain. Clouds break,
are left broken.
On the mountain plain
we wait for the horizon.

Green Tea Cooling

Noon. In the public park
there is a white scorpion
in the black knuckles
of the cherry tree.
It waits without motion
in a frail cloud of blossom.
The sun trembles
over the yellow grass.

The gardener, buckle-backed
from decades in the rice fields
takes the white scorpion
by its poised tail
smoothly and kills it
on the side of a rock
with the flat of her hand.

"I want to go North.
To Hokkaido. To see the Ainu."

"Ah, the Ainu. Our natives.
You do not see them
around here in this time.
They are all gone."

"But in Hokkaido?"

"Perhaps some, in the North.
But here they are all gone.
Like ghosts. Really,
like snow."

The Green tea cools
in our two bowls, as hours pass
in the quiet shade
of the shopfront. Outside
the traffic lessens. Noon

is almost come. The heat
reaches towards
an equilibrium. A white scorpion
waits without motion
in a frail cloud of blossom.

Jael

They came away from our mountain wars
slow with the effort of losing a country.
Foreign men, armour-hulked. Trudging, blood
on their pelts. Outsiders, and that blood
of a different making.

Animals. Kneeling to drink, dog-lipped.
Only one cupped his hands and stood. Proud
as the axis lords of Philistine. A leader,
used to strength. Though horses, men and everything
broken in the war's clumsy rout,
half-dead with knock and shield-butt.

Foreign as locusts. Still, I called him
Majesty. Sheltered him, burned olive lamps
when the day gew dim, the shouts
of troops far as Jerusalem
while the clouds skittled rain
over the scree of Ephraim.

He slept here on my bed. No doubt dreamed
of his country. Churches carved
with Baals, green-tongued. His god the demon
of noontide and scorching summers.

After, when Israel had won
its valleys and the high passes
for the goats, the orators made words of me.
They praised the power in my arms, the hands
of a hard worker, though
it was not hard to do. The tent-peg sharp,
sap-tan pine. The mallet solid yew

and he asleep, the cradle-bone
think at the temples, weak. Lank hair,
the ear full of the road of dream.
To hold the stake, mosquito-soft
and judge the blow.

No work, that—a single breath.
Lighter shift than pressing wine,
or camping on the desert plain.
The men gone and the tents to pitch.

No work. I daydream of a king's skull.
My strength, his strength, his death.
And my hands itch.

The Vampire's Price

Ladies and gentlemen, listen!
I won't be stopping here again
for quite some time and time
is precious. Name a price

for this fine ream of paper and
this splendid Tuscan alabaster.
For this brooch, carved from
the eyelid of a whale
and for this Rialto poison.

For this exquisite cat-foot
and for his nocturnal eye
and socket, fitted easily
as gloves—what am I bid? What do I hear

for prescience in fever-dreams? What price,
dear boys and girls, to have
the tungsten of the lungfish heart,
priceless, priceless—

what will I take for skylark-flight?
To catch a swift—like this!
as you might grasp a leaf
from autumn wind, if you are quick:

and how much for this key, wasp-small,
that stops the engines of the mind—
how much, to engineer desire? Pay it.
Pay it as you will.

have it all. And then,
my love, my vampire,
what will you do for me,
to live forever?

The Long Road to Silence

Only when the green river
between green trees
is left behind us
in its wrought stone

and thje wind
sheer and smooth
across worked valley earth
is left

behind and below
can the train halt
on the high plain
between the spread stances
of white mountains.

The small daughter
of the umbrella-maker
brings us tea. We sit
watching the snonw-blue moon
falling, without a word
between us.

Thinmble-small
the prayer-bell chimes
into a hot noon
without wind;

chimes again,
under the eaves,
thimble of song
filling the distances
between mountains.

Below the dunes
of snow, below this rock
rain ploughs the shining land.
Below this quiet
eagles fly,

eagles fly beneath our feet.
Silence returns
slowly as love. The green tea cools
as we wait.

The Barber's Daughter

With one clean movement
she slides the cutthroat open

with ease, as she would gut
a gulping fish. The foam
she smooths across my cheeks
is wet as sweat.

Her legs are warm
against my arm. "You shouldn't shave.
You cut yourself. You should come here
always." The knife
etches my jawline.
In the mirror

the old garage attendant
tipped back in the next chair
watches the small TV
where samurai fight
in a field of snow. Her hand is soft
as the razor. By the door

her grandfather sits in the glare
of neon and sunlight, reading
a comic book. his cheeks hollow
behind the gold dog-teeth.
When she leans close, her hair
covers my heart-beat.
"Grandfather was eaten
by the tiger-sharks
during the war."

I close my eyes. her breath
is blossom. Fingers trace
across my neck
and back. The TV
whines and shouts. Beside the door
he turns a page. Red neoon
spreads in ripples
over the silence of his face.

The Ritual of Making

"The finest cook in the province!"
her lips whisper
against a spread fan of yen.
The old women, barefoot
at the scrubbed tables
mutter at the show of money.

Over plum tea
and pickled bamboo-root
the customers up at the bar
watch him, the finest cook,
and wait. Around the chopping-board
are white spearheads of cuttlefish,
curlicues of fern and octopus,
crimson and green
in lacquer bowls. At their rims
the black resin
has worn to ochre
under his hands.

The knifepoint drums
against the board.
He rocks with it,
minutely, on the ridges
of his tiny feet. The lockjaw
of a monstrous angler-fish
is folded away smoothly
as a conjuror's trick.
his sunken eyes move to the clock
and back. the oil simmers
towards boiling-point
in a cauldron of clean steel.

"A hundred years old
or more;" my mother says;
it cold be true.
I watch the ritual
of his movement. The air
cooks slowly. Outside
the evening grows cold.

Carp pennants
bellying the wind.

Makondi Sculpture

Only the heartwood
of the ebony tree
was used. Only the heart
possesses this lacquer-lustre
and density. Under the hand,
the figure is iron-hard,

bone-thin. Slow hands
and sleepless hunger
translated this figure
from the gutteral tongue
of the ebony tree. Only heartwood:
the rest is fused with light
and softness. It has been left
to rot, or burned
under a burning sun.

Hollow as the skelton
of a vulture and winged
or spread-eagled. The form
is pmprecise. Eyeless
or eyed only with axe-strokes
that have left only
blind feature. Blind,

hungering, at its ease.
Poised, a hollowed skeleton.
A god of starvation,

blind and waiting.